VANCOUVER AND BRITISH COLUMBIA

VANCOUVER AND BRITISH COLUMBIA

CHARTWELL
BOOKS, INC.

This edition published in 2008 by

CHARTWELL BOOKS, INC.
A Division of
BOOK SALES, INC.
114 Northfield Avenue
Edison, New Jersey 08837

ISBN-13: 978-0-7858-2460-2
ISBN-10: 0-7858-2460-X

© 2008 Compendium Publishing,
43 Frith Street, London, Soho, W1D 4SA, United Kingdom

Cataloging-in-Publication data is available from the
Library of Congress

Printed and bound in China

Design: Mark Tennent/Compendium Design

The serene beauty of Whistler Mountain *(Page 2; iStockphoto 3769499 John Pitcher)*
provides a distinct contrast with the conurbation that is Vancouver
(Page 4–5; iStockphoto 5166794 Anthony Rosenberg).

Contents

Introduction

A panoramic view of the modern day Vancouver skyline at dawn *(Corbis 42-18262124 Gunter Marx/Gunter Marx Photography/Corbis).*

Introduction

A province of sublime landscapes and rich diversity, British Columbia is renowned worldwide for its breathtaking scenery, varied terrains, and copious flora and fauna. It is one of only three locations in the world which can boast temperate rainforest, but snow-capped peaks, alpine forest, azure lakes, arid desert, canyons, prairies, and tundra are also found here. In fact, British Columbia is ranked as the richest ecological area in Canada and within its lush forests live rare animals, such as the "white black bear" (a species unique to the province), the bald eagle, and the black tailed deer. The tallest trees in Canada also grow here, the Douglas fir and the Sitka spruce can reach heights of up to 295 feet (90 meters). Among these natural blessings, the people of British Columbia have built a healthy economy and cosmopolitan cities, such as the province's capital Victoria, and of course Vancouver where more than half the modern population now live.

The current border of British Columbia was established in 1846 in the "Oregon Treaty" and gives the region an area of 364,764 square miles (944,735 square kilometres), or roughly the same size as France, Germany, and the Netherlands combined. The somewhat extreme terrain has limited the amount of possible farmland; only five percent of this area is arable with sixty percent forested and seventy-five percent mountainous (at least 3,280 feet or 1,000 meters above sea level). Encompassing the areas of the Cariboo

ABOVE: The ski resort of Whistler is a popular stop for tourists and is set to hold the Winter Olympics in 2010 *(Getty 200543780-001 Getty Images/The Image Bank).*

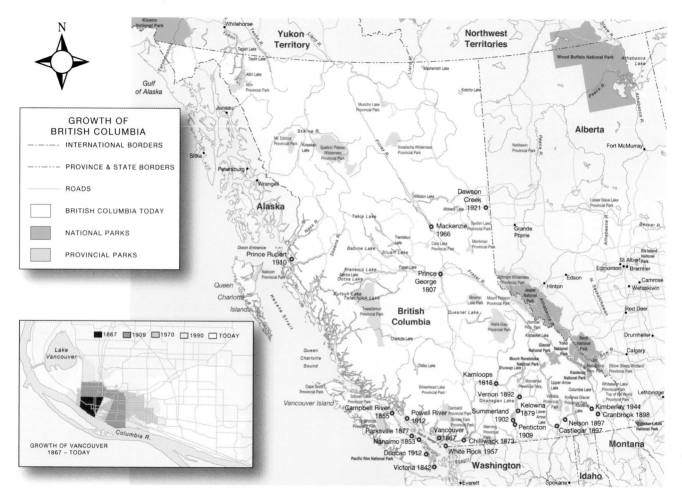

N

GROWTH OF
BRITISH COLUMBIA

- - - INTERNATIONAL BORDERS

- · - PROVINCE & STATE BORDERS

—— ROADS

BRITISH COLUMBIA TODAY

NATIONAL PARKS

PROVINCIAL PARKS

GROWTH OF VANCOUVER
1867 – TODAY

1867 1909 1970 1990 TODAY

LEFT: The Venus Mine on the Klondike Highway that runs from the Alaskan coastal town of Skagway to Yukon's Dawson City. Its route roughly parallels that used by prospectors in the 1898 Klondike Gold Rush
(Fotolia 177011 Dirk Paessler).

Chilcotin Coast, Queen Charlotte Islands, Thompson Okanagan, Vancouver Island, the Kootenay Rockies and Southern British Columbia, the region has much to offer and every part of it is unique.

Originally populated by the aboriginal people of the First Nations, archaeological findings suggest that British Columbia has been inhabited for at least 11,500 years. The first Europeans to successfully colonize the country we now know as Canada did not arrive until after 1497 when John Cabot—an Italian navigator and explorer—landed on the eastern coast and promptly claimed the land for England (though he also planted the Venetian flag). Although preceded by Spanish explorers, it was during the 1770s that the English claimed sovereignty over British Columbia following the explorations of James Cook. Finding the area rich in natural resources there was soon a healthy trade between Europeans and the artistic indigenous peoples, notably the Coast Salish, Nuu-chah-nulth (Nootka), Kwakiutl, Bella Coola, Tsimshian, and Haida. Cook was followed twenty years later by George Vancouver who charted Vancouver Island, and dispensed names to parts of the landscape, including Puget Sound and the Gulf of Georgia.

The first Europeans to arrive by overland routes were fur traders who opened trading posts as they journeyed, which were to become an established fur route. By 1821, the fur trade in the area was controlled by the Hudson's Bay Company. It is difficult now to imagine the importance of the fur trade in the nineteenth century, but at the time the beaver pelt was an integral part of fashion across Europe and Russia and the Hudson's Bay Company was rich and

RIGHT: Black Tusk, an eroded volcano peak cone, is a famous landmark above Whistler in the Garibaldi Provincial Park *(iStockphoto 5180483 Paul Morton).*

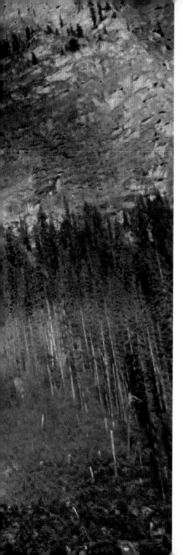

powerful enough to be the de facto government of the area. This angered American settlers in the areas that are now Oregon and Washington and in 1846 a treaty was signed that placed the border of British Columbia at the 49th parallel (with the exception of Vancouver Island).

The following decades saw a steady stream of European colonizers arriving in British Columbia. The Hudson's Bay Company founded Fort Victoria on Vancouver Island in 1843. What was to become the province's capital soon flourished and Vancouver Island's legislative assembly was established in 1856 under the Hudson's Bay official James Douglas, who became the colony's governor. Two years later the colony was flooded with prospectors headed for the Fraser River where gold had been discovered. Like other cities that became gateways to a gold rush, Victoria reaped great profits from the fortune hunters, many of whom eventually made the town their home. Today, Victoria remains the political heart of British Columbia. Walking down Victoria's Inner Harbour reveals many of the city's famous and beautifully preserved nineteenth century buildings. Perhaps the most noted of these are the Parliament Buildings. Designed by Francis Rattenbury in 1893, the domed edifice is particularly striking and even more so at night when the facades shimmer under thousands of tiny lights.

From their foothold in Victoria, the British were now eager to extend their grip over the mainland and, in 1858, established the colony of British Columbia, with its capital at New Westminster. While Douglas was appointed governor of the new colony also, the

LEFT: Takakkaw Falls in the Yoho National Park, designated a UNESCO World Heritage Site in 1984 (*iStockphoto 5212900 Rob Broek*).

RIGHT: Like most modern cities where land is in high demand, skyscrapers now dominate the Vancouver skyline *(Fotilia 3835760 cullenphotos)*.

two remained distinct until 1866, when they were united. Victoria became the official capital in 1868.

The colonists now faced a stark choice. To the east the Dominion of Canada had been established in 1867, uniting the colonies of New Brunswick, Nova Scotia, Ontario, and Quebec. To the south lay the United States. Debate as to whether to apply to be annexed by the US or to join the Dominion were fierce, but in 1871 the people of British Columbia agreed to become a part of the Dominion of Canada on the condition that they were connected to the eastern provinces by intercontinental railroad within a decade.

In fact, the railway arrived four years late, in 1885, but quickly spurred British Columbia's economic development. The province's lumber and mining industries blossomed as did farming and fishing. New settlements sprang up along the route of the railway. Its terminal—Vancouver—already an important Pacific port was further enhanced when the Panama Canal opened in 1914, opening a sea route to the eastern United States and Europe. By 1911 British Columbia's population had grown to more than 400,000, from 180,000 at the beginning of the century.

Excepting sporadic downturns, such as the Great Depression of the 1930s, British Columbia's growth proceeded at full tilt throughout the twentieth century. Highways were built and towns settled. The railways also began to spread across British Columbia,

RIGHT: A splash of summer colour surrounds this teahouse in the gardens of Victoria's Government House
(iStockphoto 2481042 Frank Leung).

notably to the Peace River District, Fort St. James, and Fort Nelson encouraging development of formerly inaccessible land. In 1951 oil and gas were found close to Fort St. John, bringing rapid economic growth and engineering projects such as the Kemano hydroelectric project, which reversed the flow of the Nechako River to power an aluminium plant at Kitimat. From the 1970s onward British Columbia began exploiting new markets for its natural wealth in the Far East, especially in Japan. In 1986 Vancouver hosted Expo '86, an exhibition devoted to the transport and communications technologies. The successful event also helped boost tourism. By the beginning of the twenty-first century the province's population had exploded to well over four million, a tenfold increase in just a century. Vancouver is also now the center of a rapidly growing high technology industry.

Today, tourism contributes a significant, and growing, amount to British Columbia's wealth. Visitors are attracted by the province's great beauty, the opportunity for outdoor sports and wilderness adventure in its national parks. Since 1985 many of these parks, including Banff, Jasper, Yoho and Kootenay, have been declared UNESCO World Heritage Sites. With its astounding natural beauty, rich history and a multi-faceted culture that stems from its original inhabitants as well as a myriad of peoples from elsewhere in the world who have all come to share in the province's bounties, British Columbia is undoubtedly "The Best Place on Earth."

RIGHT: A long pier on Vancouver Island's
Campbell River
(iStockphoto 5233440 Wendy Nero).

RIGHT: Signs like this alert hikers of the dangers of exploring the countryside of British Columbia
(iStockphoto 3695648 Adam Korzekwa).

FAR RIGHT: Heavy fog covers the lower mountain while the ski lift is bathed in glorious sunshine above Whistler
(iStockphoto 5011068 robert cocquyt).

CAUTION

ACTIVE BEARS IN AREA

PLEASE USE CAUTION WHILE WALKING:

- CARRY A BELL
- MAKE NOISE
- BE ALERT

LEFT: The Capilano Suspension Bridge, built in 1888, is 446 feet (136 meters) long and traverses almost 230 feet (70 meters) above the Capilano River in the district of North Vancouver *(iStockphoto 5127801 Klaas Lingbeek-van Kranen).*

RIGHT: The region is famed for its wines; here the wines are aging inside oak barrels *(iStockphoto 4747780 laughingmango).*

FAR LEFT: The Nitobe Memorial Garden is a traditional Japanese garden located at the University of British Columbia in the University Endowment Lands, just outside the city limits of Vancouver, and is one of the most authentic Japanese Tea and Stroll Gardens in North America *(iStockphoto 4399672 Karen Massier).*

LEFT: Vancouver's Science Center is a spectacular sight when viewed at night *(iStockphoto 2694597 Natalia Bratslavsky).*

LEFT: An aerial view of Vancouver with Stanley Park clearly visible to the top right *(iStockphoto 4840796 Dan Barnes).*

BELOW: Two apartment towers; both the Palisades on the left and the Residences on Georgia were designed by architect James Chang. The two buildings are very similar in their construction, yet distinctively different in their plan since one is oval and one is orthogonal *(iStockphoto 1443564 Niko Vujevic).*

Discovery and Pre-Confederacy (–182

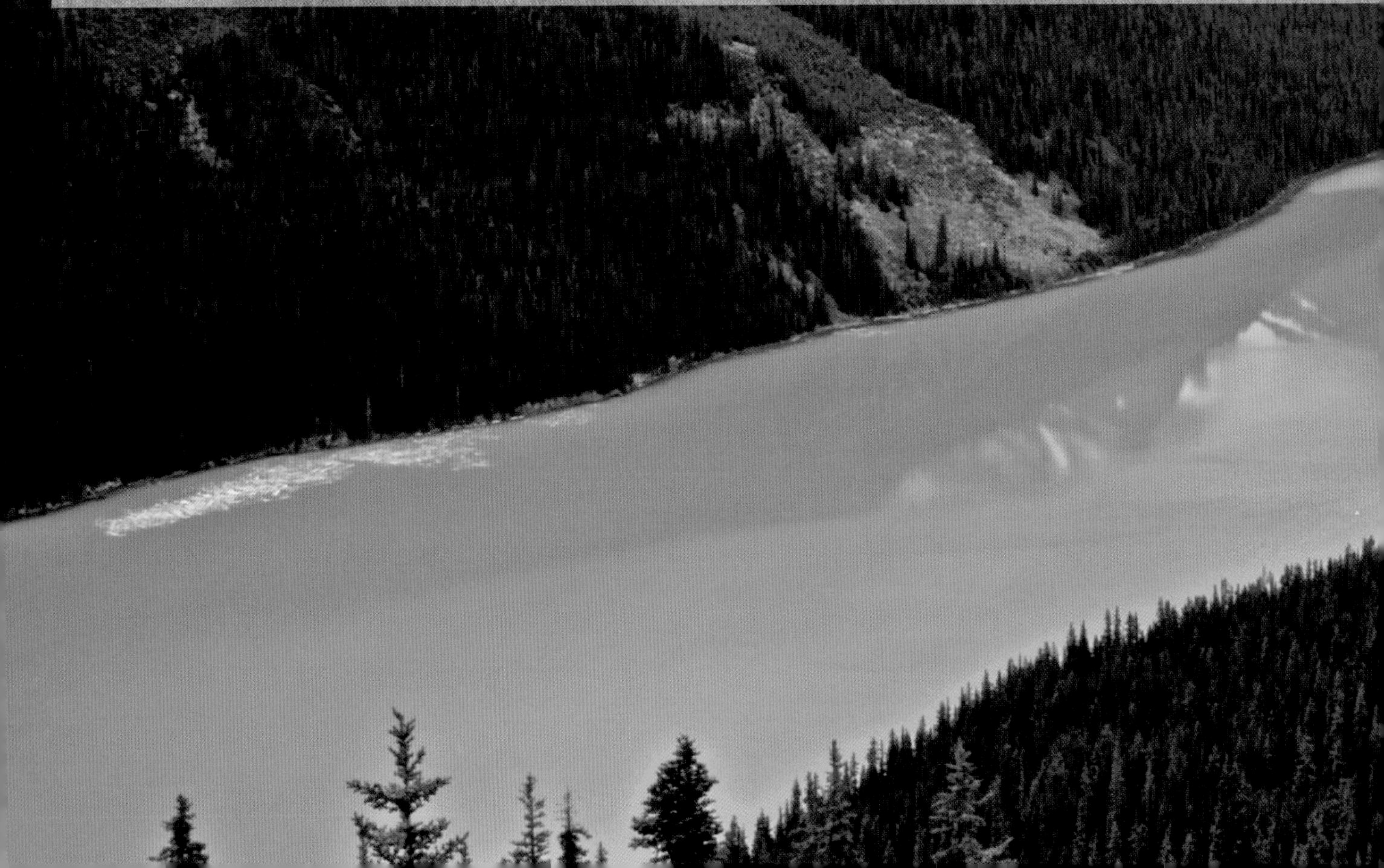

In the midst of the Banff National Park is the timeless beauty of Peyto Lake. Although British Columbia is now home to many different industries, vast swathes of its dramatic scenery remained untouched, and are the same now as would have been familiar to the distant ancestors of the aboriginal peoples *(Fotolia 748119 Natalia Bratslavsky).*

Discovery and Pre-Confederacy (–1820)

Thanks to the unearthing of ancient stone tools on the Beatton River near Fort St. John, archaeologists estimate that the region now known as British Columbia has been inhabited for approximately 11,500 years. In fact, First Nations peoples were distributed across the entire area, but settled mainly along the coast where the weather was more temperate. Due to the abundance of the forests and seas, the area contained the largest aboriginal population in the whole of Canada; when the Europeans first made contact almost half of the indigenous population of what is now Canada had settled in British Columbia.

The discoveries of James Cook and George Vancouver during the late eighteenth century saw the area around the coast and the Columbia River fall under British sovereignty. The first European to venture inland across North America to the Pacific Ocean was Sir Alexander Mackenzie. Although his expedition added to the amount of land officially under British rule, his main goal and the goal of many who followed him, was to extend the lucrative fur trade. (Fur remains one of Canada's exports to this day.) Many trading posts sprang up along his route and the two main companies—North West Company and the Hudson's Bay Company—created a permanent British presence. Some of these modest trading posts would flourish into the towns and cities that we know today. For example, Hudson's Hope (established 1805), Victoria (1843), Fort Langley (1827) and Vancouver (established 1867) all began as simple trading posts.

RIGHT: An aerial view of the Llewellyn Glacier melting into the Atlin Lake. The glacier has been supplying water to the nearby rivers for thousands of years *(Getty 78016417 J.A. Kraulis)*.

34

ABOVE: Thought to be up to 100 million years old, the Rocky Mountains in Jasper National
Park are an inspiring sight (*Fotolia 4330967 Syndac*).

Just one example of the many totem poles erected throughout Vancouver. Local parks have totems from all local tribes, Haida, Salish, Tsimshan, and Kwakiul. All along British Columbia's coast, the aboriginal peoples were, and still are today, noted as exceptional sculptors and artists. Such was the plenty of the ocean and the forests that tribes here could devote more time to cultural pursuits than elsewhere on the continent, and subsequently developed a highly sophisticated myth system as well as beautiful artworks *(iStockphoto 1802423 Jennifer Oehler).*

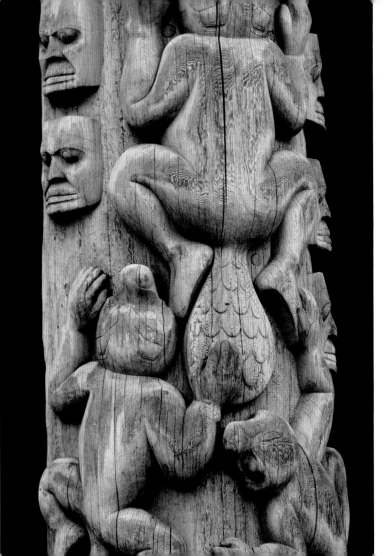

RIGHT: A close up of the intricate carvings found on a Salish tribe totem pole (*Fotolia 4636829 lev radin*).

LEFT: Called "Grandmother Tree" this ancient trunk has been carved with an intricate First Nations design *(Fotolia 2284225 amanda robinson).*

RIGHT: Although taken in the early 1900s, this photograph depicts a typical home of one of the tribes living on the prairies of British Columbia as would have been encountered by overland travelers (*Corbis IH157511*).

FAR RIGHT: Situated inside the grounds of the Museum of Anthropology is a faithful reconstruction of a Haida long house and totem poles (*iStockphoto 3040174 Phillip Jones*).

RIGHT: This very basic map shows the route taken by Captain George Dixon along the coast of the Queen Charlotte Islands in 1786–87. The paucity of detail reflects how much of the land had yet to be explored (*LoC lh000195*).

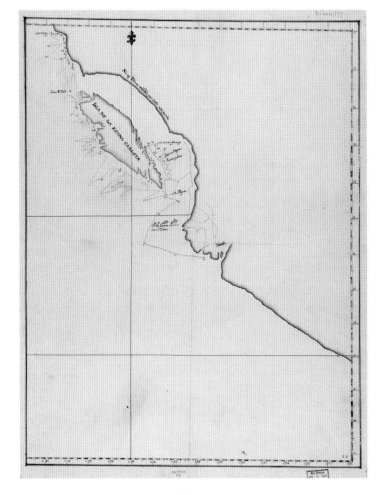

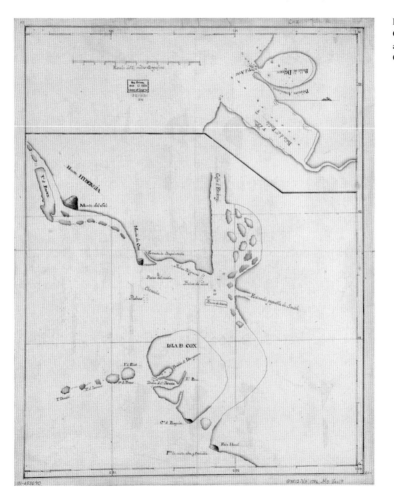

LEFT: This map shows the route taken by George Vancouver as he traversed his way across the ocean and up into British Columbia *(Loc ct00194)*.

RIGHT: A statue of the city's namesake, George Vancouver, stands outside City Hall in the heart of the city. The explorer was the first European to enter the Burrard Inlet (named for a friend of Vancouver's) on June 13, 1792, and thus into the harbor of modern-day Vancouver (*iStockphoto 4733764 Riaan de Beer*).

FAR RIGHT: Meaning "meeting of the waters" in the language of the Secwepemc tribe, Kamloops was inhabited by Europeans in 1812 when it became a modest fur trading post for the Pacific Fur Company. Nowadays it is the area's largest town (*iStockphoto 4949422 Marek Slusarczyk*).

LEFT: An illustration depicting Fort Langley on the Fraser River during the early nineteenth century. The fort dates to 1827 and was constructed to secure the Fraser River should Fort Vancouver fall to the Americans. The fort later found fortune exporting salted salmon and lumber *(Corbis BK001118)*.

ABOVE: Fur traders arrived in Vernon, originally known as Priest's Valley, in 1811. The coming of the gold rush meant the town quickly prospered and grew *(Fotolia 4252331 Ian Wilson)*.

Growth and Gold (1820–66)

An early panoramic map, drawn by
H.O. Tiedemann, showing the landscape
of Victoria on Vancouver Island in 1860
(LoC pm010750).

Growth and Gold (1820–66)

Following the amalgamation of the two main fur companies in 1821, the area now known as British Columbia was split into three departments—New Caledonia, Columbia District, and Athabasca District. These three boroughs were given the generic title of "British North America" and left to the management of the Hudson's Bay Company. However, as American settlement progressed, so too did disputes over territory. Those settlers to the south whose fathers had already successfully won independence from Britain were ill-disposed to be governed by a British company. These problems were solved in 1846 by the Oregon Treaty, which divided the land across the 49th parallel all the way to the Georgia Straits. Everything to the south became part of the United States (excepting Vancouver Island, part of which falls below the 49th parallel) and everything to the north became "New Caledonia." The colony of Vancouver Island was established in 1849 and Victoria named its capital. A legislative assembly was appointed in 1856 under company official James Douglas, who also became governor of the Colony of British Columbia when the mainland colony was established in 1858.

All this was to change following the Fraser Canyon Gold Rush of 1858 and the Cariboo Gold Rush of 1862. Suddenly the administration faced an influx of thousands of Americans. Entire towns such as Bakerville and Atlin appeared overnight and the makeshift government strived to meet the needs of its massively

ABOVE: This sketch of Fort Vancouver shows the city as it was in 1845 when it was just a burgeoning fur trading post *(Corbis IH158899)*.

growing population. The Vancouver Island colony was also straining under increasing financial pressure and the two provinces eventually merged in 1866. Queen Victoria named the new united territories "British Columbia."

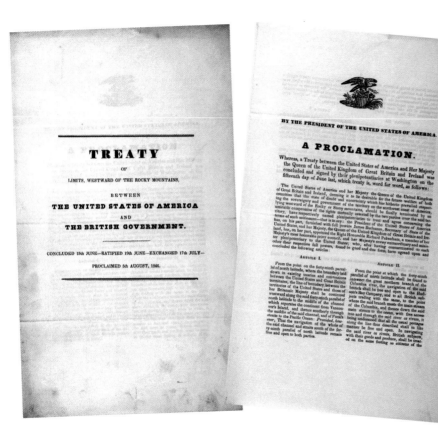

ABOVE, CENTER, RIGHT: A copy of the 1846 Oregon Treaty which set the borders for British
Columbia and the United States *(LoC treaty1,2,3).*

FAR LEFT: This is the Hudson's Bay Trading Post of Fort Shepherd. Built in 1857 it was an important stop for those traveling to the Kootenay gold rush sites. It burned down in 1872 and is now the site of a conservation park *(LoC 08569u)*.

LEFT: This church, built in 1858 in Victoria is a typical example of some of the first buildings to be found on the island *(LoC 08566u)*.

LEFT: The Fort Langley National Historic Park has preserved and restored many old cabins dating back to its first British settlers in 1858 (*Corbis MX001912 Gunter Marx Photography/Corbis*).

ABOVE: Nestled between the Fraser Valley and Mount Baker is the city of Abbotsford. The development of Abbotsford began after the area was surveyed following the Gold Rush in 1858 (*iStockphoto 4296763 Lijuan Guo*).

LEFT: This early photograph shows a view of Fort Victoria as it was in 1859 when it was just beginning to grow *(LoC 08562u)*.

ABOVE: Esquimalt village in 1859. This township on the southern tip of Vancouver Island provided an alternative to Victoria Harbor and was frequently used to offload cargoes *(LoC 3g11405u)*.

ABOVE: The view of a newly formed Victoria Harbor on Vancouver Island as it was back in 1859 *(LoC 3g11407u)*.

RIGHT: An early photograph of the Fort Vancouver Trading Post in 1860 *(LoC 3g11409u)*.

FAR LEFT: Virtually unchanged since its construction in 1860, the Fisgard Lighthouse was the first of its kind to be built on the west coast of Canada *(iStockphoto 1531984 Jason van der Valk).*

LEFT: A gold mine in the 1800s. Thousands of people flocked to Northern Canada during the Klondike gold rush in the Yukon and then the Fraser Canyon gold rush in British Columbia *(Corbis BE053460 Bettmann/Corbis).*

FAR LEFT: The view out over the Columbia River looking toward Vancouver in 1860 (*LoC 08570u*).

LEFT: The small gold and silver mining town of Rock Creek in 1860. Located in Boundary Country in Southern Okanagan, this small settlement soon became a boomtown (*LoC 3g11433u*).

ABOVE: Once on a trading route for the Squamish and Lil'wat tribes, Whistler was discovered by Europeans in 1860. Named after the mating call of the native hoary marmot, Whistler is now a popular ski resort *(iStockphoto 836701 Ronnie Comeau)*.

RIGHT: Bastion Square was originally built during the boom of the mid to late nineteenth century and contains many of Victoria's oldest buildings including the impressive MacDonald Block tower *(Getty Images 78016522 Chris Cheadle)*.

ABOVE: This illustration depicts the early settlements of Vancouver when it was still a burgeoning trading post (*Getty 74596090 Paolo Fumagalli*).

RIGHT: One of the early churches built on Vancouver Island. This church and its graveyard has been lovingly preserved (*Getty Images 6077-002879 Doug Plummer*).

RIGHT: Not all of Vancouver's old churches have been saved from the ravages of time. This century old church has been left to ruin *(Fotolia 3147707 Andy-Kim Möller)*.

FAR RIGHT: The awe-inspiring mountains of Williams Lake supply a changeless background for these men herding cattle. British Columbia's gold rush precipitated a large growth in farming, in order to feed the many thousands of prospectors headed to the gold fields
(Corbis OR008848 Charles O'Rear/Corbis).

Confederation (1867–1914)

The Banff Springs Hotel was the brainchild of William Cornelius Van Horne, manager of the Canadian Pacific railroad, who built this baronial styled edifice in 1888 to take advantage of the nearby hot springs and the tourists they attracted *(Fotolibra FOT84668 Geoffrey Lipscombe).*

Confederation (1867–1914)

The Dominion of Canada was formed in 1867 through the uniting of three other British North American colonies. At that time British Columbia was facing financial breakdown. In the wake of the gold rush huge population growth and the desperate need for government funded services had given rise to enormous debt, and many felt that the route to stability lay in unification with either the United States to the south, or Canada to the east. When the new Canadian government agreed to take on the territory's debt and lay the Canadian Pacific Railway into British Columbia, Canada gained its sixth province on July 20, 1871.

The Canadian Pacific Railway was completed in 1885 and gave the economy of British Columbia a much needed boost. Now the transportation of its many resources to the east could begin. Along the route of the railway new settlements sprang up and, as British Columbia's population grew, so too did industry and agriculture.

Alongside such rapid growth and industry came the need for a larger work force. To remedy the matter, immigrants were invited to British Columbia from Europe, China, and Japan. Unfortunately, it

RIGHT: Gastown in Vancouver is named after "Gassy" Jack Deighton, a sailor from England who was famous for his ability to chatter and for the saloon he opened here in 1867
(*Fotolibra FOT64886 Philip Gordon*).

LEFT: An example of the beautifully preserved nineteenth century architecture remaining in Vancouver's "Gastown" area *(Fotolibra FOT170535 Mervyn Benford).*

was not long before the local population grew resentful of the new settlers and riots ensued. Many Chinese and Japanese workers were attacked in Vancouver in 1887 and 1907 which led the government to put a stop to further immigration. Despite these problems, industry in British Columbia expanded and in 1914 the second transcontinental railway, the Grand Trunk Pacific, was completed.

ABOVE: Chinatown in Vancouver dates back to well before the city became the sprawling metropolis it is today. Immigrant Chinese workers first came to this area in 1858, lured by stories of gold and riches. The area was named as an historic site in 1977 and restoration began in earnest (Getty Images 71627461 Lawrence Worcester).

RIGHT: A panoramic view over Victoria in 1878. The small provincial town would soon develop into a bustling capital city (LoC pm010760).

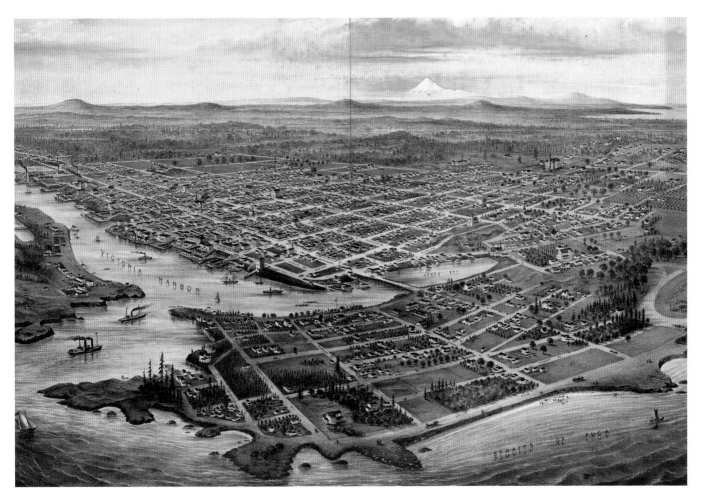

ABOVE: A selection of Victoria's most popular attractions adorn this poster, dated 1884 *(LoC pm010761)*.

RIGHT: This panoramic map shows Victoria in the year 1889. Comparing this map with the previous illustration from 1878, it is easy to see how the island city has developed *(LoC pm010770)*.

VICTORIA, B.C.
1889.

LEFT: Built in the 1870s and erected on the corner of Victoria's Water and Cambie streets, the famous steam clock was the first of its kind *(iStockphoto 3337397 zennie)*.

ABOVE: A monumentous moment in British Columbia's history was captured on film in 1885. Here, Donald A. Smith drives in the very last spike of the transcontinental railroad *(Corbis BE061444 Bettmann/Corbis)*.

ABOVE: This tranquil scenery can be found within Vancouver's first park. Stanley Park was opened in September 1888 and covers an area of 400 hectares (*Fotolia 2229280 Robert Lickley*).

RIGHT: Victoria's streets lined with nineteenth century architectural gems are redolent of the city's history. Craigdarroch Castle was built by local coal millionaire, Robert Dunsmuir, in 1889 (*Fotolia 5199409 wellesenterprises*).

ABOVE: One of the oldest landmarks in Victoria, Market Square is beautifully preserved and now has a range of modern shops and museums dedicated to the history of the island *(Getty Images 56619068 Alan Marsh).*

Above: An alternative view of Market Square, Victoria, built during the 1880s boom period (*Getty Images 56619070 Alan Marsh*).

LEFT: Standing on the edge of Lake Louise in the Rocky Mountains is the Chateau Lake Louise Hotel. Dating back to 1894, it is still a hugely popular spot for tourists more than a century later *(Fotolibra FOT120032 Mike Reed, arps).*

ABOVE: The mining town of Atlin appeared in 1898 following the Atlin Gold Rush. Originally from the Tlingit language "Äa Tlein" meaning "large body of water" it referred to the nearby Atlin Lake *(Corbis BRK582 Photo Collection Alexander Alland Sr./Corbis).*

LEFT: Encircled by the Canadian Rockies, the city of Fernie was founded in 1898. It is the largest and oldest community in this area
(Getty Images 78175900 Ellen Atkin).

RIGHT: The Holy Rosary Cathedral once dominated the skyline of Vancouver. Work began in 1899 and it opened for its first mass on December 8, 1900
(Fotolia 367703 Volodymyr Kyrylyuk).

Butchart Gardens in Victoria began life
in 1904 as a limestone quarry but under
the ministrations of Jennie Butchart was
transformed into an amazing landscape
of ornamental gardens
(iStockphoto 121120 Marje Cannon).

ABOVE: The impressive Fairmont Empress Hotel is one of Victoria's most famous landmarks. It was completed in 1905 and designed by Vancouver Island's favourite architect, Francis Rattenbury *(iStockphoto 3236914 constantgardener)*.

RIGHT: Once a courthouse, this building is now home to the Vancouver Art Gallery. Designed in 1906 by Francis Rattenbury, the gallery boasts a permanent collection of 8,000 works of art *(Fotolia 4884744 Askander)*.

FAR LEFT: An aerial view over Gastown.
It is possible to see in the foreground the
Dominion Building. Built in 1906, it was
Vancouver's very first high rise and on its
completion was the tallest building in the
British Empire
(Fotolia 1390463 dave timms).

LEFT: A close up of the Dominion Building.
Sadly, the architect of this famous tower,
J.S. Heyler, died after falling down the
front staircase soon after it was opened
*(Corbis MX006299 Gunter Marx
Photography/Corbis).*

FAR LEFT: Located in Colwood, Vancouver Island, and built in 1906, Hatley Castle was later selected as home to Queen Elizabeth and her daughters, Margaret and Elizabeth, during the Second World War. However, it was decided that the departure of the Royals to a place of safety would damage British morale
(Getty Images 78016519 Chris Cheadle).

LEFT: The Sinclair Building was completed in 1910 and originally housed the main post office. Nowadays the gorgeous Baroque construction houses an exclusive shopping mall
(iStockphoto 4921122 Riaan de Beer).

RIGHT: Russian settlers, known as Doukhobors, work on one of the many co-operative farms found in Kootenay in 1910 *(Corbis SF37670 Bettmann/Corbis).*

FAR RIGHT: The idyllic town of Telegraph Cove was established in 1912 on the north side of Vancouver Island. The town was built on stilts over the water with boardwalks between each building. *(Corbis NF004024 Natalie Fobes/Corbis)*

The Sun Tower with its recognizable green dome (seen in reflection) was built in 1912 and overtook the Dominion Building as highest tower *(Fotolia 81561 Volodymyr Kyrylyuk)*.

Esquimalt was inhabited by the First Nations for 400 years before the arrival of the Europeans. It was incorporated as a city in 1912 and is now one of British Columbia's busiest ports *(iStockphoto 1353113 Steve McBeath)*.

Wartime and Depression (1914–1950)

Logging has always been an important industry in British Columbia. In the early 1900s oxen were used to haul logs to the Royal City Mills camp just outside Vancouver (*Corbis FCC-F-018141-000 Alinari Archives/Corbis*).

Wartime and Depression (1914–1950)

After the First World War, and following intense social problems caused by heavy drinking, British Columbia embraced Prohibition—though not for long. Returning veterans put pressure on the government and the rules were subsequently altered so that soldiers and working men could relax with a drink. However, the United States kept the stringent anti-booze laws and thanks, in part, to copious cross-border smuggling, British Columbia continued to prosper. Vancouver in particular owed much of its wealth to the "outlaw economy."

It is no surprise then that when US prohibition was repealed the economy of British Columbia began to suffer and the arrival of the Great Depression saw the province's ebullient growth evaporate. Vancouver was put under particular strain as tens of thousands of men flocked to the city to find work. Giant "hobo jungles" grew up around False Creek and the railroads. In these desperate times the government was often forced to take extreme measures. Martial law was imposed on the docks for three years and when a group of men occupied the main Post Office at Granville and Hastings, the police were sent in to violently end their protest.

Everything changed with the advent of the Second World War and its aftermath. Women began to contribute to the work force as never before, Canada's army and navy grew to be the third largest in the world, and finally the economy began to strengthen.

RIGHT: Still one of the most important industries in British Columbia, these felled trees at Prince George await transportation to the mills
(Corbis LM001923 Dan Lamont/Corbis).

LEFT: At the beginning of the twentieth century, parts of British Columbia remained uncharted and explorers continued to mount expeditions to its more remote corners. This picture, taken in the early 1900s at Alert Bay on Cormorant Island, depicts two typical Nimkish totem poles *(LoC 3a47176u)*.

LEFT: Taken in 1914, this photograph depicts a typical Nimkish Village of that era *(LoC 3c11295u)*.

ABOVE: In 1924 Byron Harman and Lewis Freeman led an expedition over the great British Columbian ice fields. This one hundred and fifty square mile area was virtually unknown and uncharted before *(Corbis HU035248 Hulton-Deutsch Collection/Corbis).*

RIGHT: Prince Rupert, once a small railroad town, was incorporated in 1910 and is now the second largest port town on British Columbia's coast. Surrounded by forests and mountains it manages to retain its old world charm *(Corbis NF119045 Natalie Fobes/Corbis).*

RIGHT: Tourism in British Columbia is not a recent development. In this 1927 photograph travellers to Lake Windermere sleep outside the train carriage due to the oppressive heat inside the train *(Getty Images HS1983-001 Topical Press Agency)*.

FAR RIGHT: The Marine Building—seen to the far left of this picture—no longer dominates the skyline as it did on its completion in 1930. It remained the tallest building in Vancouver for nine years *(Fotolia 3234613 Sarah Evans)*.

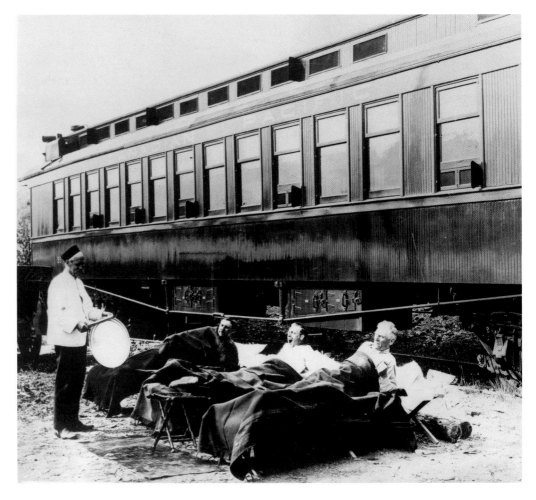

ABOVE: Construction of the Lion's Gate Bridge in Vancouver began in 1937 and was completed just over a year later. The building work provided many jobs during the Depression *(iStockphoto 4872051 Volodymyr Kyrylyuk).*

LEFT: Douglas Street in British Columbia's capital city, Victoria, in 1939. Very few of the buildings in this picture remain standing today *(Corbis HU045442 Hulton-Deutsch Collection/Corbis).*

RIGHT: The Fairmont Hotel Vancouver was opened in 1939 and is actually the third hotel in Vancouver to take this name. The first, built in 1916, served as an army barracks during the Second World War and was then demolished in 1949. The second was one of the most lavish hotels in all the British Empire, boasting ballrooms, lounges, and gold-plated bathroom fittings *(Getty Images 200188237-001 Amanda Marsalis)*.

FAR RIGHT: Looking out across Downtown Vancouver in 1939 to the Marine Building and False Creek in the distance. Many of these quaint commercial buildings would soon be replaced with huge skyscrapers *(Corbis U506105ACME Bettmann/Corbis)*.

The Burrard Street Bridge was built in 1942 and joins downtown Vancouver to Kitsilano—the neighbourhood on the west side of the city *(Fotolia 2169401 Kwest)*.

RIGHT: This illustration, dating to 1946, shows the Marine Building on Vancouver's Hastings Street. Once the tallest building in the vicinity, it is already dwarfed by the surrounding skyscrapers that denote British Columbia's soaring post-war economy *(Corbis LW002067 Lake County Museum/Corbis)*.

Hastings Street and Marine Building,
Vancouver, B. C., Canada

RIGHT: This picture was taken two days after work began on the Alaska Highway in 1942. Altogether it took eight months and twelve days to complete *(Corbis BE036534 Bettmann/Corbis).*

FAR RIGHT: Today the Alaska Highway stretches 1,488 miles (2,344 kilometers) through forests, mountains and wilderness *(Corbis MX006458 Gunter Marx Photography/Corbis).*

FAR LEFT: This photograph shows the famous "Signpost Forest" on Watson Lake. Begun in 1942 by a soldier who was homesick for Danville, Illinois, it now has over 10,000 different signs (*Corbis U1312596INP Bettmann/Corbis*).

LEFT: Established as a trading post in 1850, Nanaimo is now the second largest city on Vancouver Island. This picture shows the Marina as it was in 1947 (*Corbis BR001497 Ray Krantz/Corbis*).

Post War to Present Day (1950–2008)

Post War to Present Day (1950–2008)

Following the end of the Second World War, British Columbia—already growing in economic strength and confidence—began to blossom. A discovery of natural gas and oil deposits in 1951 near Fort St. John boosted the economy a great deal. In 1964, the railway reached out as far as Fort St. James in the interior, finally making vast tracts of unused land available for logging and mining. During the 1960s, the Premier, W.A.C. Bennett, began a series of development programs, including the agreement between British Columbia and the US to build four hydroelectric dams along the Columbia River. He also improved and expanded the transportation system, founding BC Ferries, and building new highways and bridges. This helped open up the rest of British Columbia to the world and tourism began to play a crucial economic role. Vancouver and Victoria became important cultural centers as writers, poets, actors, dancers, gourmet chefs and great thinkers were all drawn to the cities, tempted by the warm weather and spectacular scenery.

RIGHT: This photograph taken in 1954 shows a typical Vancouver street scene. The towering skyscrapers are not yet apparent and the city still retains some of its old world charm *(Corbis U1063377 Bettmann/Corbis)*.

FAR RIGHT: An aerial view of Vancouver's complex railway network in 1964. These huge yards take British Columbia's many exports directly to all major shipping lanes *(Corbis U1446825 Bettmann/Corbis)*.

Closer trade links with nearby Japan helped British Columbia's economy to grow even stronger during the 1970s. One company signed an agreement to export 50 million tons of coal to Japan over the following 15 years.

In 1986, Vancouver hosted the hugely successful Expo '86. A showcase for communication and transport technologies, it also helped boost tourism to the area, as did the new highways stretching into Kamloops and the Okanagan Valley.

In 2000, British Columbia signed a monumentous agreement with the Nisga'a people. The Nisga'a Treaty granted them 775 square miles (2,007 square kilometers) of land, cash and benefits, plus the right to govern themselves. It was an historic agreement and has paved the way for more of its kind. Currently there are 50 other groups looking to negotiate a similar treaty with the government.

RIGHT: Vancouver in 1966 had the busiest docks in the western world and was well on its way to becoming Canada's third largest city (*Corbis U1537554 Bettmann/Corbis*).

FAR RIGHT: The distinctive Vancouver Museum and Pacific Space Center was built in 1967. The design of the roof is based on the shape of a First Nations hat (*Corbis 42-17478134 Rudy Sulgan/Corbis*).

ABOVE: Although Vancouver has had a Museum of Anthropology since 1947, this particular building was not completed until 1976. The design is inspired by the architecture of the First Nations long house architecture *(Corbis MX006757 Gunter Marx Photography/Corbis).*

RIGHT: Once a poor industrial area, Vancouver's Granville Island has been redeveloped since the 1970s. Now the island has brightly painted studios, galleries, shops and a popular market *(Corbis 42-17477520 Rudy Sulgan/Corbis).*

FAR LEFT: Downtown Vancouver and the Harbor Centre Tower. One of the best known attractions in Vancouver, the centre was officially opened in 1977 by Neil Armstrong. His footprint was encased in cement and is now on display in the observation deck *(iStock 2763988 Volodymyr Kyrylyuk).*

LEFT: A close up of the Harbor Centre Tower at night. It looks all the more remarkable when illuminated *(Fotolia 5999240 Anthony Rosenberg).*

LEFT: A modern civic centre and beautifully designed public plaza, Robson Square was completed in 1983. It connects Robson Street to the Vancouver Art Gallery *(Fotolia 651919 fred goldstein).*

ABOVE: The futuristic geodesic dome that now houses Vancouver's Science World was first built for the 1986 Expo by R. Buckminster Fuller *(iStock 592184 Michael Puerzer).*

ABOVE: The view across the water of the distinctive dome of Science World.
The center is famous for its Omnimax cinema located at the pinnacle of the dome
(Getty Images 73251803 DEA/M.BORCHI).

ABOVE: Resembling a line of moored yachts, Canada Place was built to house Canada's exhibitions for Expo '86. It now holds a hotel, conference centres and a terminal for cruise ships *(Fotolia 836737 Volodymyr Kyrylyuk)*.

LEFT: A close up on the impressive roof "sails" of the building at Canada Place *(Fotolia 3891110 Volodymyr Kyrylyuk)*.

ABOVE: The Skytrain in Vancouver opened in time for Expo '86 and is statistically one of the safest ways in the world to travel. During its entire history there has not been one collision or derailment *(Getty Images 5662072 Ken Straiton)*.

ABOVE: Yaletown in downtown Vancouver was once overrun with unattractive warehouses and rail yards but since the 1986 World's Fair it has been transformed into one of the most desirable neighborhoods in Vancouver *(Getty Images 56619377 Ken Straiton).*

RIGHT: Vancouver Public Library was erected in 1995 and cost 106 million CAD to complete. It currently holds nearly 1.5 million items and makes eight million loans per year *(Fotolia 5103556 fred goldstein).*

LEFT: Named after a discovery of coal deposits found in 1862, Coal Harbor has been redesigned as a high class, high rise apartment district since the 1990s *(Getty Images 200533130-001 Raimund Koch).*

ABOVE: The west end of Vancouver at sunset with majestic Mount Baker dominating the background *(Getty Images 56619113 Alan Sirulnikoff).*

LEFT: Imposing skyscrapers tower over Burrard Street, now the center of the financial district of downtown Vancouver *(Getty Images 57020253 Ruth Tomlinson).*

ABOVE: Just next door to Canada Place is this open air meeting place. Many people stop here to enjoy the views over the water *(Getty Images 71626901 David Tomlinson).*

The view looking down modern day
Hornby Street, Vancouver
(*Getty Images 73026066 Panoramic Images*).

LEFT: The curiously shaped One Wall Center is presently the tallest building in Vancouver with a height of approximately 492 feet or 150 meters *(Fotolia 557609 fred goldstein).*

RIGHT: An aerial view of Kelowna, Okanagan. Now the area's largest city and famous for its flourishing wine industry, Kelowna was first inhabited by missionaries in 1859 *(Fotolia 4279765 Ian Wilson).*

RIGHT: Newly planted vines line the cliffs in Penticton alongside the Okanagan Lake. This area now has a flourishing wine industry and organizes an extremely popular peach festival every year *(iStock 4392373 laughingmango).*

FAR RIGHT: Looking out across the docks in Victoria, when compared with the photograph from the previous century, it is easy to see how much the city has grown and changed *(iStock 3334983 Andrew Penner).*

LEFT: Named for a Spanish mathematician and scientist, Tofino—on the west coast of Vancouver Island—is a popular tourist destination. During the summer its population swells with surfers, hikers, and whale watchers
(Getty Images 56619071 Alan Marsh).

FAR LEFT: A typical example of the many modern apartment blocks now lining the streets of downtown Vancouver (*iStock 3993955 Adam Korzekwa*).

LEFT: Facing inland, modern day Howe Street, next to Canada Place, is a sea of glass towers where there were once small nineteenth century houses and shops (*Fotolia 4897109 Askander*).

A view down modern day Granville Street. Modern high rise buildings have replaced the nineteenth century architecture seen in the previous chapter (*Getty Images 76134972 Robert Postma*).

RIGHT: Here in downtown Vancouver it is rare to see an older building amid a forest of new and glittering skyscrapers (*Fotolia 4897121 Askander*).

ABOVE: The revitalizing of Vancouver continues with the government breathing new life into many areas, even the tunnels are given a new coat of paint *(Fotolia 763728 Terry Alexander)*.

RIGHT: An aerial shot of the modern day city of Vancouver *(iStock 4367357 Niko Vujevic)*.

Index